GRADUS

MUSIC ANTHOLOGY
BOOK II

GRADUS

MUSIC ANTHOLOGY

BOOK II

---

by Leo Kraft

PROFESSOR OF MUSIC, QUEENS COLLEGE OF THE CITY UNIVERSITY OF NEW YORK

W. W. Norton & Co., Inc., New York

to the memory of Paul Klapper

Copyright © 1976 by W. W. Norton & Company, Inc.

First Edition

Library of Congress Cataloging in Publication Data

Kraft, Leo.
  Gradus.

  Includes bibliographies.
  — —Music anthology.
  1. Music—Theory. 2. Music—Analysis, appreciation.
I. Title.
MT6.K877G7 Class suppl: MT6.K877G7Suppl. 781 75–40207
ISBN 0–393–09197–X (Anthology II)

Book design by Hermann Strohbach

Printed in the United States of America

1 2 3 4 5 6 7 8 9

CONTENTS

GRADUS

MUSIC ANTHOLOGY

BOOK II

Models of imitation
from *The Art of Counterpoint*

Gioseffe Zarlino   1558

Examples

from Playford's *Introduction to the Skill of Music*   Henry Purcell   1694

1.

Fuge in the Fourth below *

2. Per Arsin & Thesin

Imitation by inversion

3. Augmentation

Diminution!

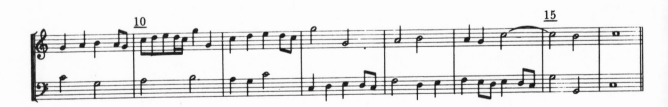

* By "Fuge" Purcell means imitation.

Examples *from Rules of Counterpoint*   J. P. Sweelinck   c. 1600

1. Imitation a 4th lower

2. Inversion of 1

3. Imitation a 5th higher

4. Inversion of 3 (complete!)

5. Imitation at the octave by inversion

6. Imitation at the 5th by inversion

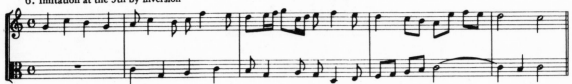

100D

Verses of the Magnificat Chant
in organ setting

Antonio de Cabezón c. 1550

MAGNIFICAT CHANT

Three Imitations for organ

Salvatori 17th century

101A

Canon at the Octave for two voices from
Playford's *Introduction to the Skill of Music*　　　Henry Purcell　1694

Canon in the 8th or 15th

101B

Canon at the Unison from *Pamelia*　　　William Byrd　1609

The Fourth Commandment
Canon at the Unison for four voices   Franz Joseph Haydn   1791

101D

Canon

at the Unison for four voices K. 553

Wolfgang Amadeus Mozart   1788

1. Al - - - - - le - lu - ia, al -

2. - - - - - - - - - - le - lu - ia,

3. al - - - - - - - - - le - lu - ia,

4. al - le - lu - ia, A - - - - men. Al - le - lu - ia.

Canon at the Unison for four voices

Ludwig van Beethoven 1812

1. Tick - a tock - a, tick - a tock, tick - a tock, tick - a tock, tick - a tock _____ Mael - zel, you are a gen - ius;

2. Tick - a tock - a, tick - a tock, in - ven - tor great are you!

3. Tick - a tock - a, tick - a tock, Now time al - ways will be meas - ured by your met-ro-nome, tick - a

4. Tick - a tock - a, tick - a tock - a, Ev - 'ry-one will count with you, with the met - ro - nome, tick-a tock, tick-a

This humerous canon was written by Beethoven in honor of his friend Maelzel, the inventor of the metronome.

Canon

at the Unison for three voices Op. 113 No. 12

Johannes Brahms 1891

Benedictus

Orlando di Lasso   c. 1560

S
Be - - - ne - di - ctus, _____ qui ve - - - - - - - - -

A
Be - - - ne - di - ctus, _____ qui ve - -

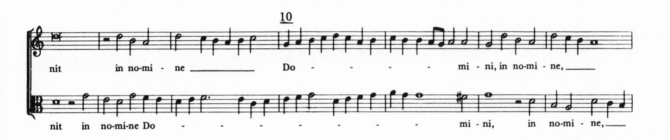

nit in no-mi - ne _____ Do - - - - - - mi-ni, in no-mi - ne, _____

nit in no-mi-ne Do - - - - - - - - mi - ni, in no-mi - ne, _____

in no-mi - ne, _____ in no-mi - ne _____ Do - - - mi - ni.

_ in no-mi - ne, _____ in no-mi - ne _____ Do - - - - mi - ni.

103

Chanson

Claude de Sermisy   c. 1560

S: Pit - y on me for all I must en - dure

A: Pit - y on me for all I must en - dure

To serve you though I want it

To serve you though I want it not,   I

not

want it   not,

For Love can make you

For Love can make you   love as

love   as   I

I

do;   And make you pay   the price   for   your   past   cru - - - -

do; And make you pay the   price for your past   cru - - - - - - - el -

14

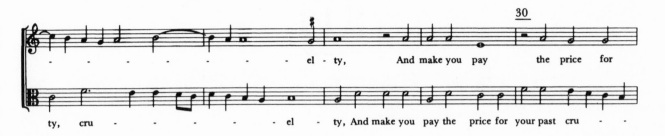

el - ty, And make you pay the price for

ty, cru - - - - - el - ty, And make you pay the price for your past cru - -

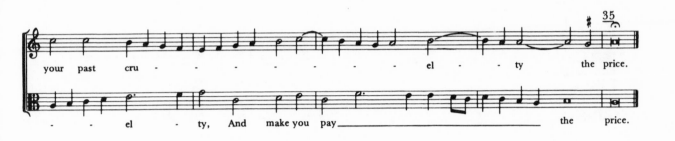

your past cru - - - - - - - - el - ty the price.

- - el - ty, And make you pay_____ the price.

Sanctus

Johannes Ockeghem   c. 1475

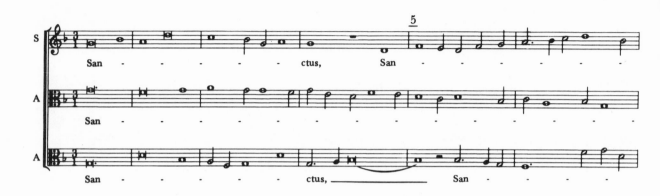

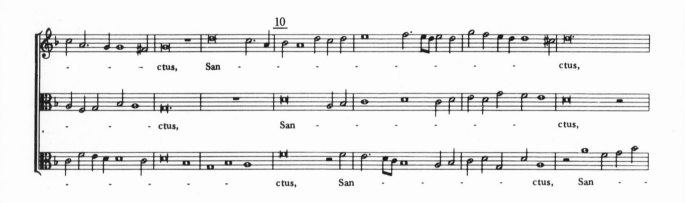

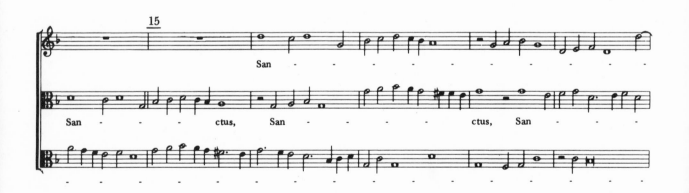

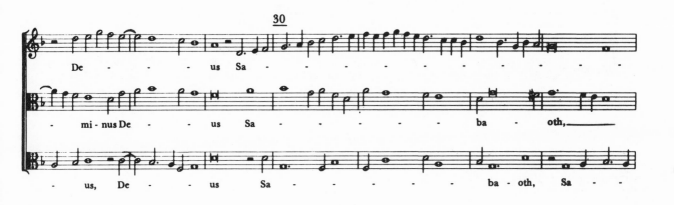

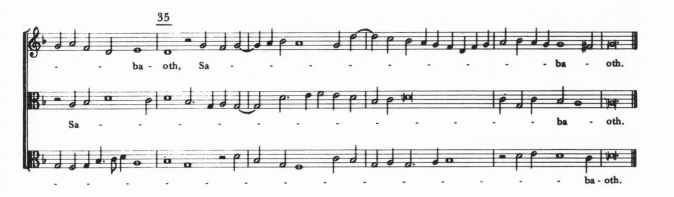

105

Motet: *Puer natus est*

Christóbal Morales   1543

So Light Is Love

John Wilbye   1609

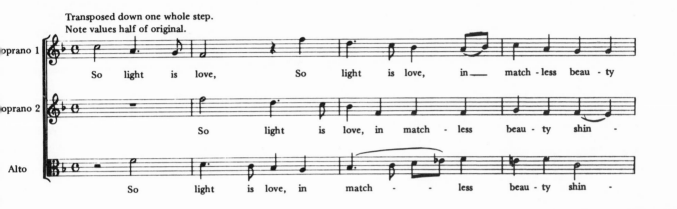

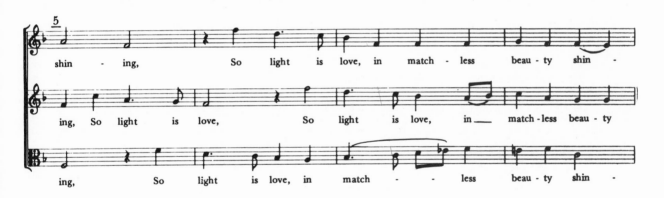

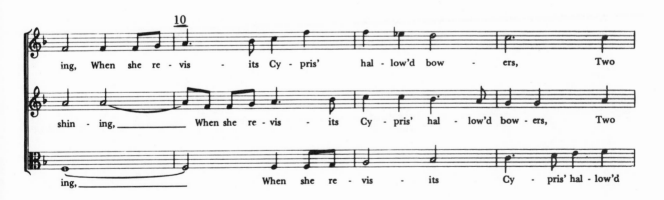

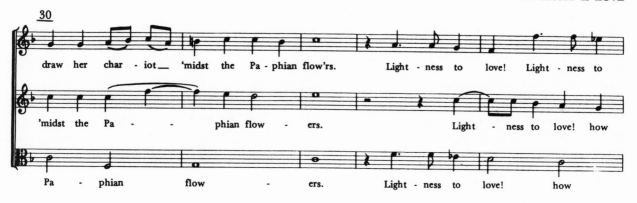

draw her char - iot___ 'midst the Pa - phian flow'rs. Light - ness to love! Light - ness to

'midst the Pa - - - phian flow - ers. Light - ness to love! how

Pa - phian flow - - ers. Light - ness to love! how

love! how ill it fit - - - teth, Light - - ness to

ill it fit - teth, Light - - ness to love! Light -

ill it fit - teth, Light - - ness to love! how

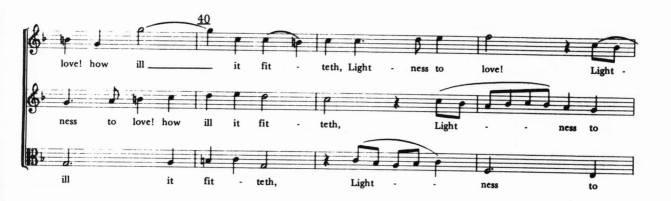

love! how ill_____ it fit - teth, Light - ness to love! Light -

ness to love! how ill it fit - teth, Light - - ness to

ill it fit - teth, Light - - ness to

- - ness to love! how ill it fit - teth, So

love! Light - - ness to love! Light - ness to love! how ill it fit - teth, So___

love! how ill it fit - teth, how ill_____ fit - teth, So

23

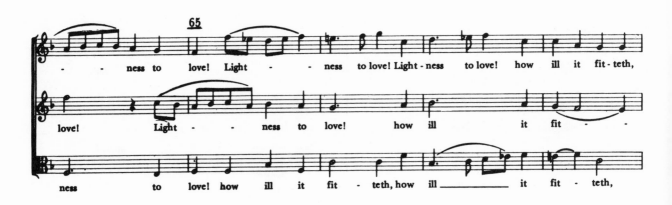

107

Chorale from Cantata No. 38   Johann Sebastian Bach   1724

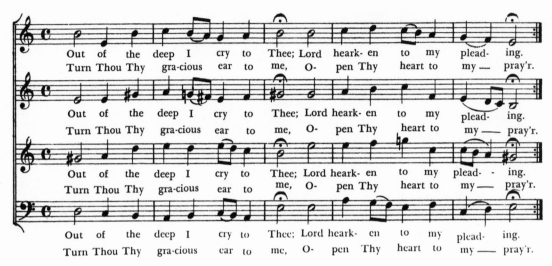

Out of the deep I cry to Thee; Lord heark- en to my plead- ing.
Turn Thou Thy gra-cious ear to me, O- pen Thy heart to my pray'r.

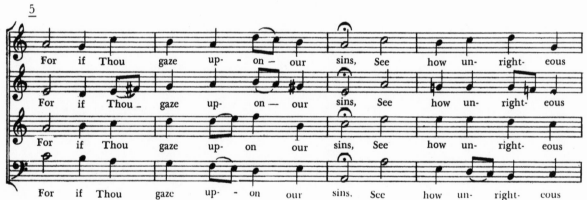

For if Thou gaze up- - on - our sins, See how un- right- eous

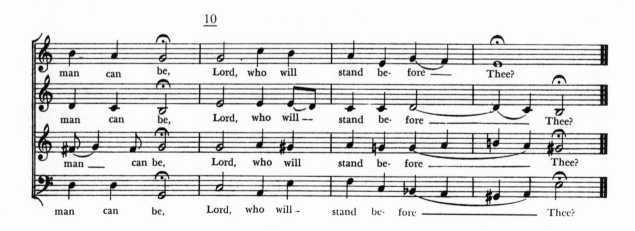

man can be, Lord, who will stand be- fore Thee?

108

Chorale from Cantata No. 20

Johann Sebastian Bach   1724

28

109

Chorale from Cantata No. 81

Johann Sebastian Bach 1724

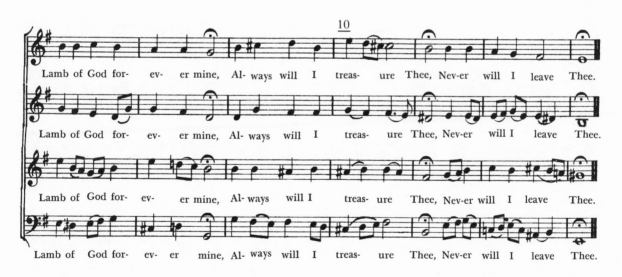

O World, I Now Must Leave Thee

from *St. Matthew Passion*   Johann Sebastian Bach   1729

Chorale from Cantata No. 90

Johann Sebastian Bach 1723

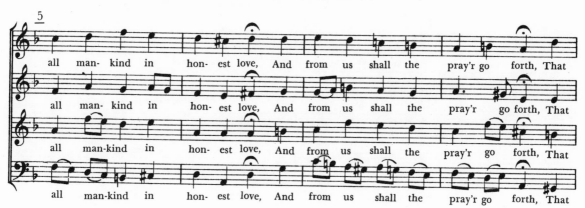

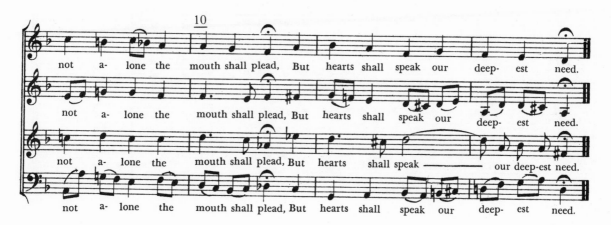

112A

Chorale from Cantata No. 148   Johann Sebastian Bach   1725

112B

Chorale from Cantata No. 5

Johann Sebastian Bach 1724

Chorale from Cantata No. 172

Johann Sebastian Bach 1714

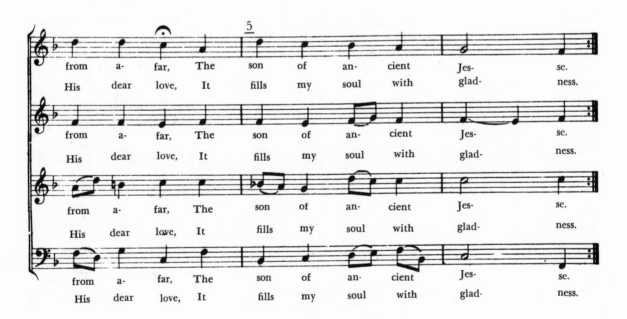

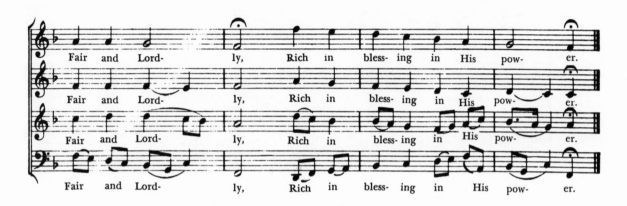

Chorale from Cantata No. 43

Johann Sebastian Bach 1726

115

Our Father

J. P. Sweelinck   c. 1600

Compare this setting with Telemann's on the same melody, [120], and Buxtehude's, [121].

Christ Lay in the Bonds of Death

from the *Gorlitz Organ Book*

Samuel Scheidt   1650

We Are All Mortal
from the *Little Organ Book*

Johann Sebastian Bach   1717

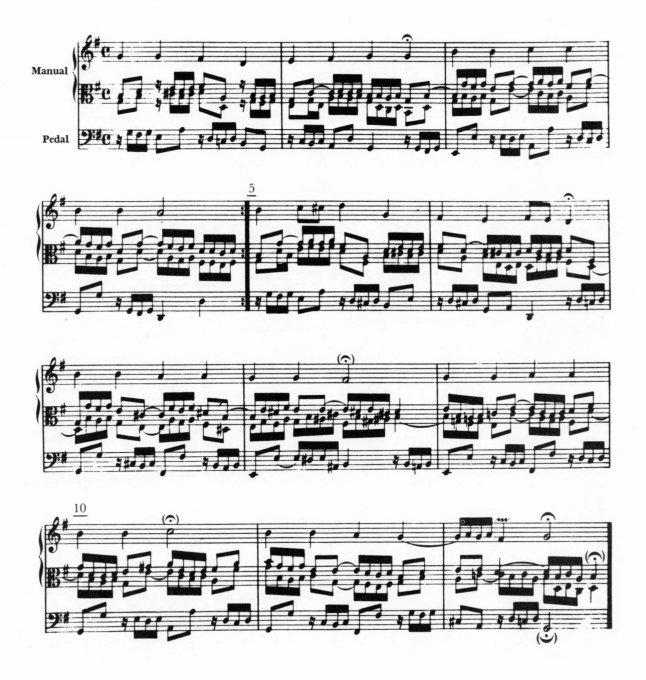

In Dulci Jubilo

from the *Little Organ Book*

Johann Sebastian Bach   1717

119

O World, I Now Must Leave Thee

Op. 122

Johannes Brahms   1896

The melody is that of Isaac's *Innsbruck*, 45. It is also the tune set by Bach in the chorale 110

120

Our Father

G. M. Telemann   c. 1750

121

Our Father

Dietrich Buxtehude 1746

This is the same chorale melody that is used in 115 and 120.

Before Thy Throne I Stand

Johann Sebastian Bach 1750

Kyrie

Tomás Luis de Victoria   1592

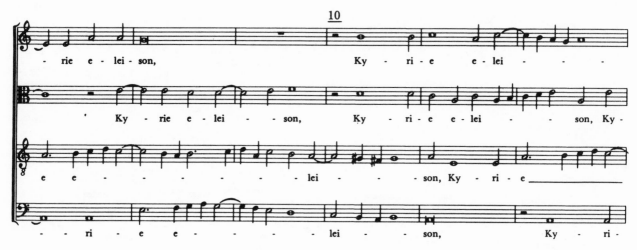

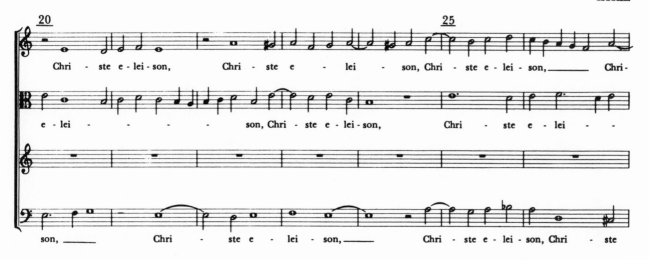

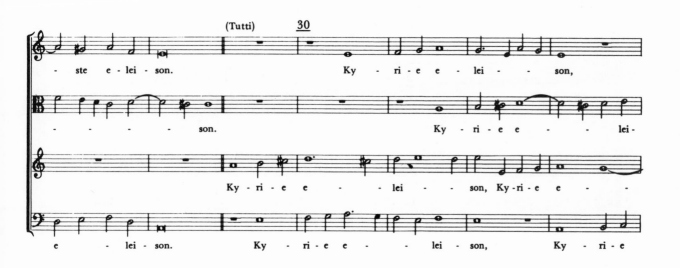

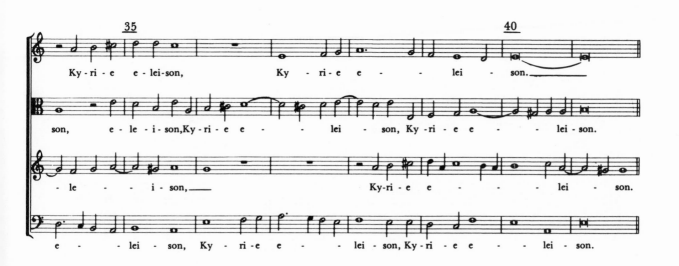

Kyrie from the Mass *Pange Lingua*   Josquin des Pres   1539

Kyrie from the *Mass for Five Voices*

William Byrd   1588

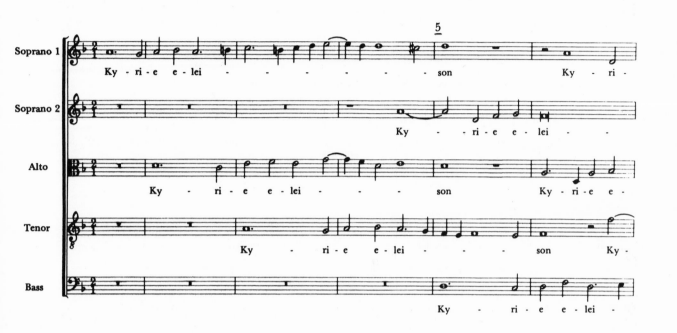

123D

Kyrie
from the *Pope Marcellus Mass* Giovanni Pierluigi da Palestrina 1567

From the *Opere Complete di Giovanni Pierluigi da Palestrina,* vol. 4, pp. 167 ff., edited by R. Casimiri and published by L'istituto Italiano per la Storia della Musica, Rome, with whose permission it is reproduced.

75

124

Ricercare for instruments

Andrea Gabrieli   1589

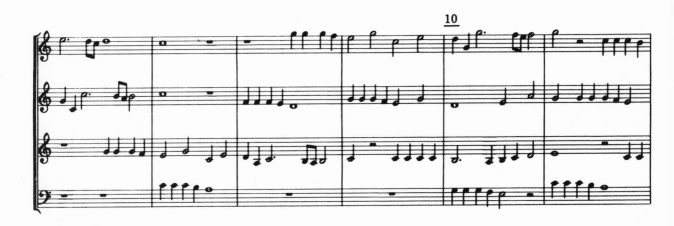

The original title of this piece is "Ricercare in the Twelfth Mode." However, the piece corresponds to the definition of a *canzona*—that is, the tunes are lively, the piece is sectional, and the opening section is repeated near the end.

62

Fantazia for viols

Henry Purcell 1680

Fugue

Guillaume Gabriel Nivers   1667

127

And With His Stripes from *Messiah*   George Frideric Handel 1741

Prelude and Fugue in C minor
from *The Well-Tempered Clavier*, Book I

Johann Sebastian Bach   1722

Three Contradanses

Ludwig van Beethoven   1802

129A

The country dance or contradanse was popular in England, France, and Germany in the eighteenth century.

129B

Beethoven used this idea in three other works: the ballet music for *Prometheus*, the *Variations for piano* Op. 35, and the last movement of the *Eroica Symphony*.

129C

Six Waltzes Op. 9a

Franz Schubert   1816–19

130A

130B

130C

130D

130E

130F

Pantomime

from *Orfeo ed Euridice,* Act 2, Scene 2   Christoph Willibald Gluck   1762

The marking "Violoncelli" in 5 means that the cellos play, the basses do not. "Tutti" in 7 means that both play.

Violoncelli.   Tutti.

132

Sonata Op. 14 No. 2,
second movement

Ludwig van Beethoven   1799

Andante.
La prima parte senza replica.

133

Symphony No. 104, Minuet and Trio   Franz Joseph Haydn   1795

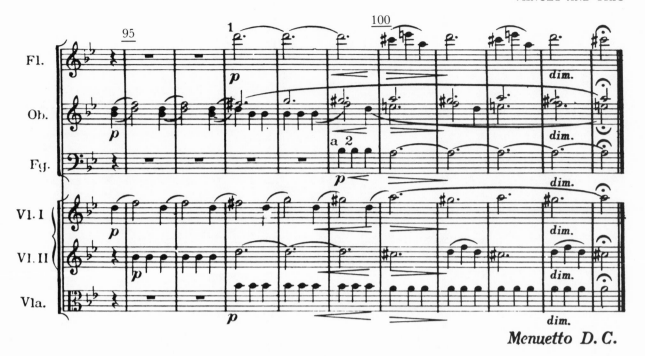

134

Minuet K. 94

Wolfgang Amadeus Mozart 1770

String Quartet in D Minor K. 421,
Minuet and Trio

Wolfgang Amadeus Mozart   1784

Menuetto D.C.

String Quartet

Op. 18 No. 2, Scherzo and Trio

Ludwig van Beethoven   1800

Wind Quintet Op. 88, No. 3, Scherzo   Anton Reicha   1820

138

Sonata Op. 50 No. 1
Adagio, mm. 1–26

Muzio Clementi   c. 1800

Aveu from *Carnaval* Op. 9

Robert Schumann   1834

139B

Chiarina from *Carnaval* Op. 9

Robert Schumann   1834

54338

Echoes from the Theater

from *Album for the Young* Op. 68
Robert Schumann   1848

Quintet for Clarinet and Strings Op. 115,

second movement, mm. 1–41   Johannes Brahms   1892

142A

Theme
from *Thirty-two Variations in C Minor* Ludwig van Beethoven 1807

142B

Sonata Op. 53, *Waldstein,*
first movement, mm. 1–13 Ludwig van Beethoven 1804

Facsimile of the Beethoven autograph: *Waldstein* Sonata, second movement, opening measures. (See top of facing page.)

142C

Sonata Op. 53, *Waldstein,*
second movement, mm. 1–9

Ludwig van Beethoven   1804

143

Rondo in A Minor K. 511,
mm. 1–8

Wolfgang Amadeus Mozart   1787

The autograph of Prelude Op. 28 No. 1 with the dedication by Chopin to his friend J. C. Kessler discernible in the upper right hand corner.

Prelude Op. 28 No. 1

Frédéric Chopin   1838

144B

Prelude Op. 28 No. 4   Frédéric Chopin   1838

Prelude Op. 28 No. 5

Frédéric Chopin 1838

Allegro molto

Chopin's autograph of Prelude Op. 28 No. 9. At the bottom right is the composer's instruction to the engraver to add the octave notes in the bass wherever the number 8 appears.

Prelude Op. 28 No. 9

Frédéric Chopin 1838

Prelude Op. 28 No. 17

Frédéric Chopin 1838

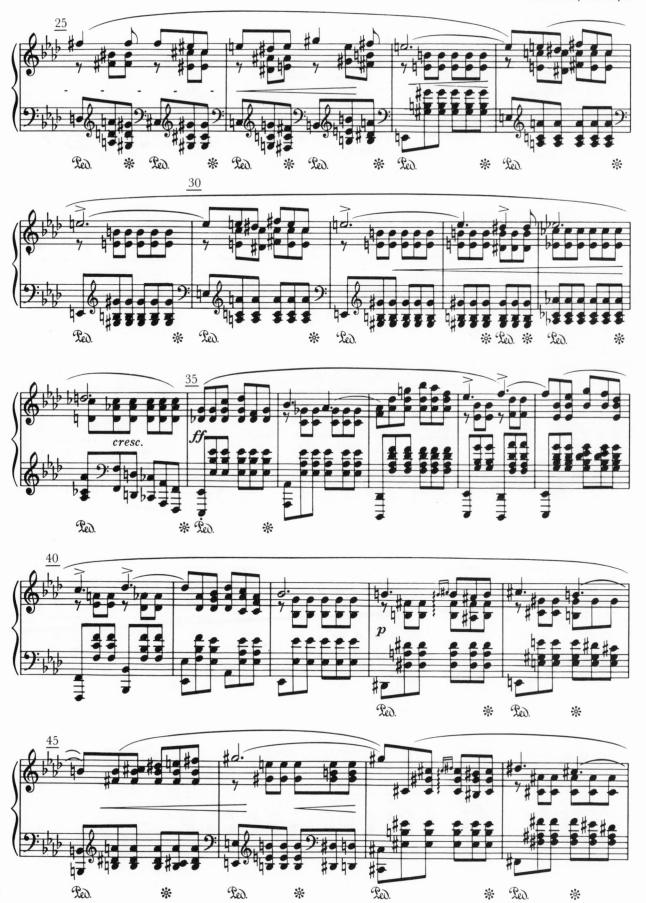

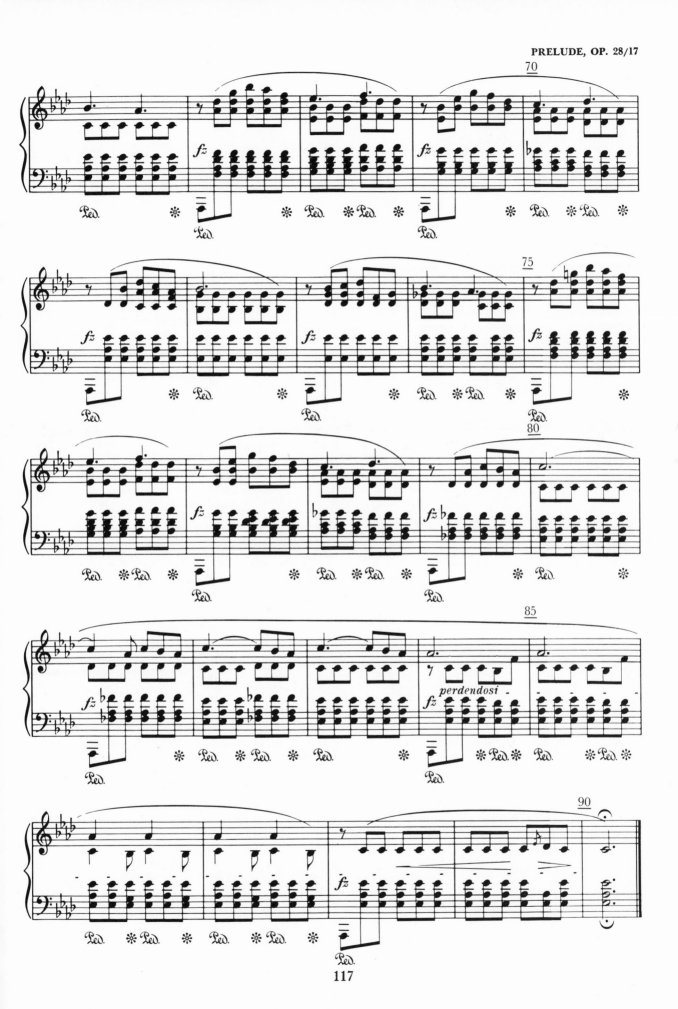

Autograph of Prelude Op. 28 No. 20, in which the ending is extended by four measures. In the note to the publisher marked with an asterisk, Chopin explains that this is a little concession to a "Monsieur X," who is often right.

Prelude Op. 28 No. 20

Frédéric Chopin 1838

Prelude Op. 28 No. 22

Frédéric Chopin   1838

144H

Mazurka Op. 6 No. 1, mm. 1–40

Frédéric Chopin 1832

12 Variations on *Ah vous dirais-je, Maman*

K. 265　　　　　　　　　　　　　　　　Wolfgang Amadeus Mozart　1778

Variations on a Waltz by A. Diabelli

Op. 120: theme, variations 1, 2, 3, 8, 9   Ludwig van Beethoven   1823

Var. I
Alla Marcia maestoso

Var. II
Poco allegro

Var. III
L'istesso tempo

Var. IX
Allegro pesante e risoluto

147A

String Quartet Op. 74 No. 3,
second movement

Franz Joseph Haydn   1793

String Quartet Op. 76 No. 1, Minuet — Franz Joseph Haydn 1795

Etude Op. 10 No. 3

Frédéric Chopin 1830

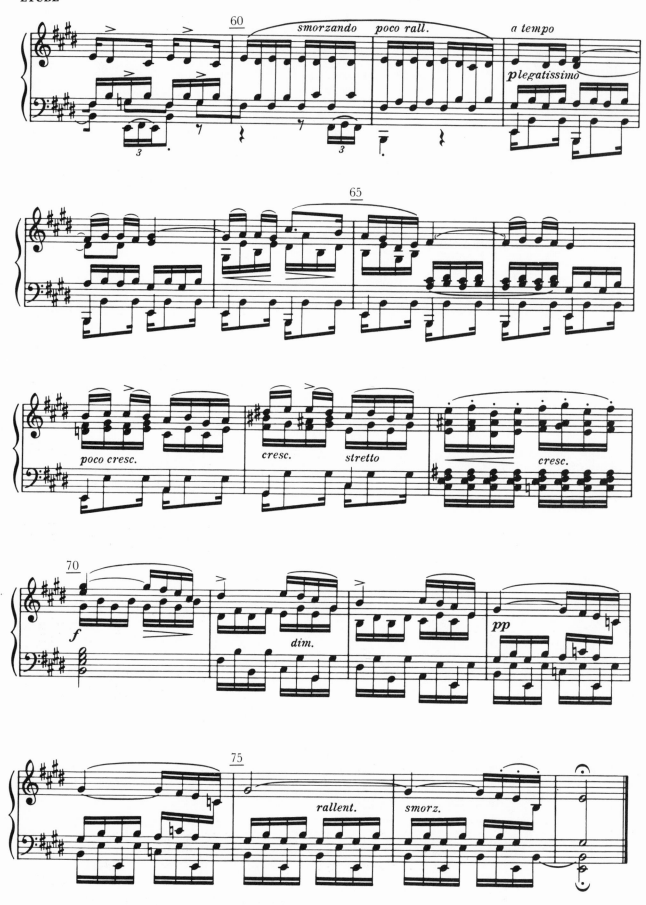

Il Penseroso

Franz Liszt 1839

The title of this piece refers to a statue by Michelangelo which impressed Liszt deeply. The composer appended to the music a quatrain written by the sculptor, in which the statue seems to say that it is grateful to be made of stone because of the injustice that is on earth.

The Longing One *from The Miller's Fair Daughter*

from the German of Wilhelm Müller   Franz Schubert   1823

I Really Cannot Believe It
from *A Woman's Life and Love*

from the German of Adalbert von Chamisso   Robert Schumann   1840

153

New Love Op. 19 No. 4

from the German of Heinrich Heine

Felix Mendelssohn c. 1830

O Death Is Like the Cooling Night Op. 96

from the German of Heinrich Heine

Johannes Brahms   1886

O death is like the cool- ing night, But life is as the sul- try day. Now dark-ness comes; I'm drow- sy; The day has so wea- ried me.

154

Nocturne Op. 43 No. 2
from the French of Villiers de L'Isle-Adam

Gabriel Fauré 1886

155

Prison Op. 83 No. 1
from the French of Paul Verlaine

Gabriel Fauré 1900

156

Mignon from the German of Goethe

Hugo Wolf   1888–89

One of the most influential works of early Romanticism is the novel *Willem Meister's Year of Wandering* by Goethe (1749–1832). This poem is included in the novel. The same lines have also been set by Beethoven, Tchaikovsky, and others.

Death's Lullaby *from Songs and Dances of Death*

from the Russian of Golenischtschev-Kutusov   Modeste Moussorgsky   1875

Lento funesto.

"Do not be fright- ened, my friend! See the spring morn-ing shines in- to your win-dow.

You are so wea- ry, so sad, now shed no more tears. Put

sor-row be-hind you; Let me watch here by my-self.

171

dreams of pleas-ure and joy I will bring him. Lull- a- by, boy, lull- a- by."

"Wait, now, have pit- y on him, stop —— your sing- ing, Stop that sad tune that you

sing!" "Look you, how sweet- ly he sleeps in his cra- dle. Lull-a- by, boy, lull-a- by."

Aria: *Dalla sua pace*

from Act 1 of *Don Giovanni* K. 527 — Wolfgang Amadeus Mozart 1787

I sigh—then with her, and mine her sad ness, and mine her weep-ing, and I'm not hap- py

if she is not, I can't be hap-py If she is not, I can't be hap-py If she is not.

I love her dear-ly, My life de- pends on hers, What makes her hap- py — brings me the same joy, What makes her

sad, — makes me to die, makes ——— me wish to die. What her hap-py, me the joy love her
makes brings same I

dear-ly, I love her tru-ly, What her sad, —— makes me to die, makes —————— me wish to —— die.
makes

What her makes me to die, —— makes me to die.
makes sad,

159

Quartet from Act 3 of *Rigoletto*

Giuseppe Verdi 1851

Fair-est daughter of the Grac - es, I, thy humble slave, im - plore thee, With one ten-der word to joy re - store __ me, End the pangs, the pangs of un - re-quit - ed love. Of my

anguish see the traces, Thee I treasure all a - bove, ___ With one

tender word to joy re - store ___ me, End the pangs, the pangs of un - requit - ed

Gilda.

Maddelena.
Ah! to speak of love thus

Duke. I appre-ciate you right-ly, All you say is but to flatter.

lar.
love.

light - ly! **Maddelena.**

Ah, I laugh to think how man - y Yet your ten - der tale may

strove,   for he   is false,   my heart   is

laugh,   I   ap - pre - ci - ate you right - ly, all you say is but to

love,   Of   my__ an - guish   see   the

prove.   The   strength   to

cresc.

bro - ken, ah,   in vain   for bliss   I strove, ah, _____ in

flatter, ah, I laugh to think how many yet your tender tale may move, yes,   yes,

trac - es,   thee I treasure   all   a - bove ah,   yes,

pun - ish   shall   not   fail   me,

f

190

Excerpt from Act 1 of *Otello*

Giuseppe Verdi   1887

Flower Song from Act 2 of *Carmen*

Georges Bizet 1875

Through ev-'ry long and lone-ly hour — In pris-on there, — I kept your flow — er, And though its bloom — was swift-ly gone Its haunt-ing fra — grance lin-gered on. In the dark-ness, as — I lay dream — ing, Its per-fume, con-sol-ing, re-deem — ing, Re-

called your im - age night and day, And my de - spair —— would fade a -

way. —— An - oth - er time,— I would be - rate you, I

swore to de - test — and to hate you! Of what Nem - e - sis —— am I the

prey?— What whim of fate — sent you my way? —— Then

es Cast a ___ spell ___ a - round my

heart, Lur - - - ing me on like an en - chant - ress.

You ruled my soul! You took pos-session of my heart!

Car - men, I love _____ you!

Symphony No. 1 Op. 21,
first movement

Ludwig van Beethoven 1799

The autograph of the same recitative from Handel's *Messiah* that appears on the facing page in a contemporary edition.

163

Thy Rebuke Hath Broken His Heart
from *Messiah*

George Frideric Handel   1742

164

Symphony in B Minor

(*Unfinished*), second movement, mm. 197–end   Franz Schubert   1822

165

Two Excerpts from *Romeo and Juliet*

a. mm. 175–191

P. I. Tchaikovsky   1879

b. mm. 484–509

Symphony in D Minor,

first movement, mm. 1–12

César Franck   1888

Elsa's Dream,
excerpt from Act I of *Lohengrin*

Richard Wagner   1848

167B

Wotan's Farewell,
excerpt from Act 3 of *Die Walküre*

Richard Wagner   1856

Closing Scene from Act 2 of *Parsifal*

Richard Wagner   1882

167D

Prelude

to Act 1 of *Tristan und Isolde,* mm. 1–10

Richard Wagner 1859

Liebestod,
Closing scene from *Tristan und Isolde*

Richard Wagner 1859
Piano transcription by Franz Liszt 1874

The tremolos should be *ppp*, very slurred, and with the greatest number of notes possible.

Die Begleitung immer sehr ruhig und *pp*

Sehr weich.

Sehr weich.

234

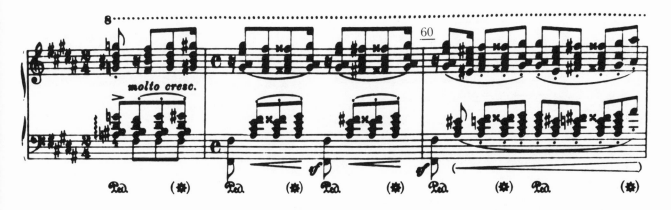

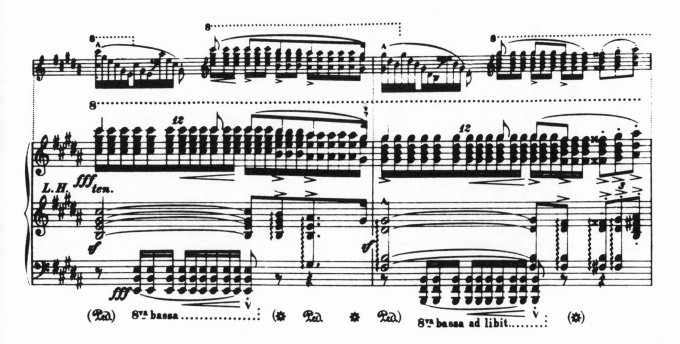

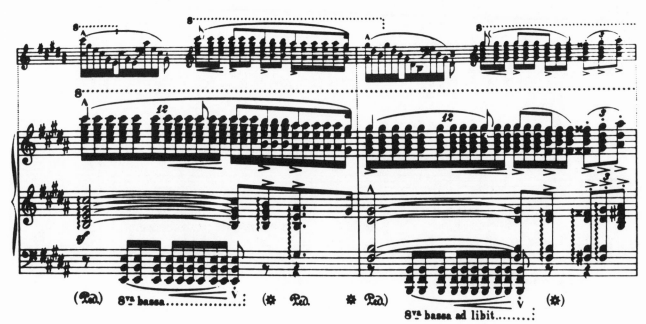

169

Song Op. 2 No. 2
from the German of Mombert

Alban Berg   1908

'Tis the Ecstasy of Languor

from the French of Paul Verlaine

Claude Debussy   1888

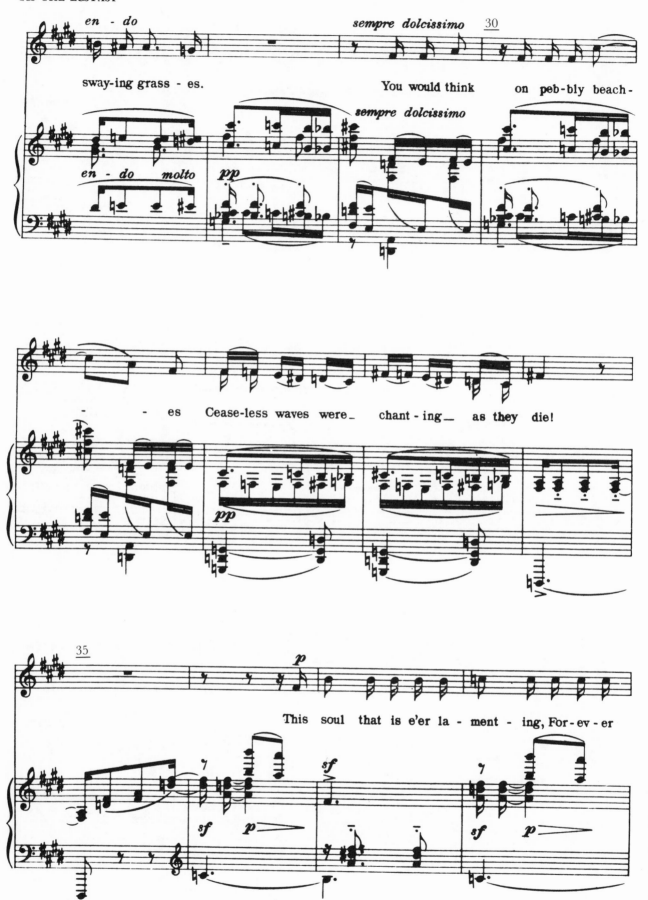

La Soirée dans Grenade

Claude Debussy   1903

Mouvement de Habanera

Commencer lentement dans un rythme nonchalamment gracieux

PIANO

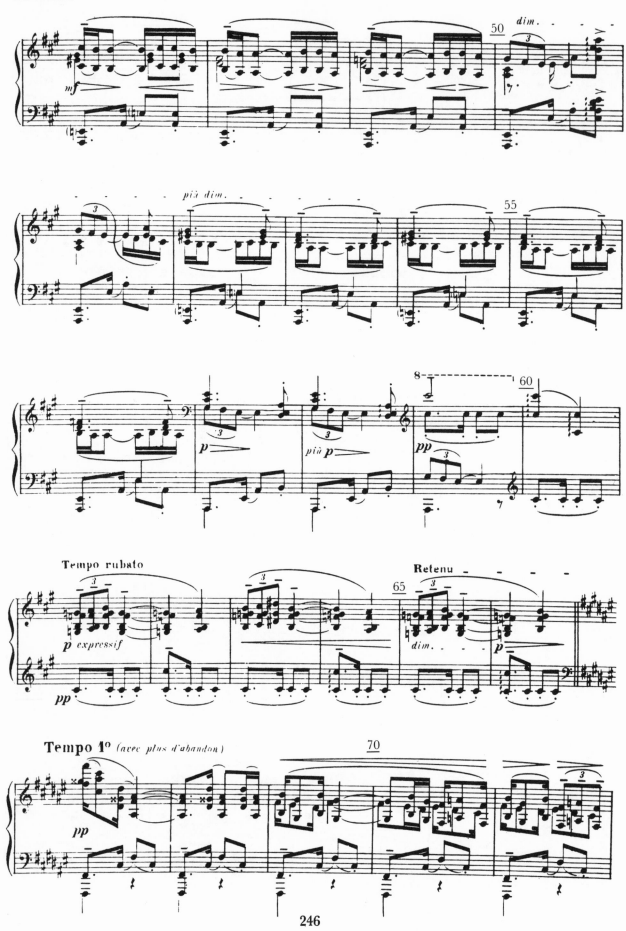

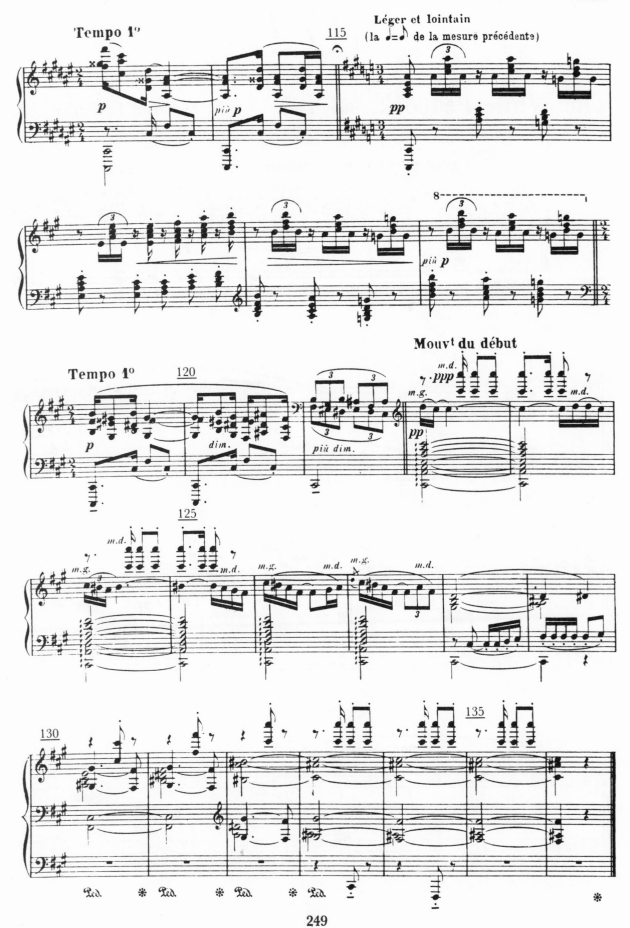

The White Peacock, mm. 1–18

Charles T. Griffes 1915

Languidamente e molto rubato

Afterglow

Charles Ives   1919

The piano should be played as indistinctly as possible, and both pedals used almost constantly.

174A

No. 100: In the Style of a Folk Song
from *Mikrokosmos*

Béla Bartók   1936

No. 102: Harmonics from *Mikrokosmos*   Béla Bartók   1936

𝅗𝅥, 𝅘𝅥 **Press down keys without sounding**

174C

No: 125 Boating from *Mikrokosmos* Béla Bartók 1936

No. 132: Major Seconds Broken and Together

from *Mikrokosmos*

Béla Bartók   1936

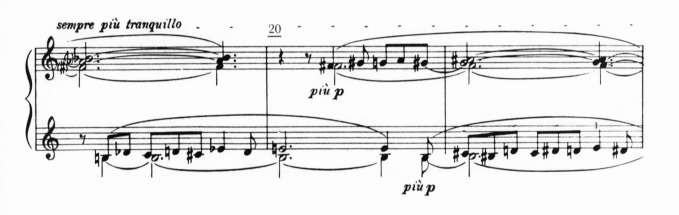

No. 141: Subject and Reflection

from *Mikrokosmos*

Béla Bartók   1936

175

Part Two, Introduction,

from *The Rite of Spring*
Arranged for two pianos by the composer.

Igor Stravinsky   1913

176

Symphony of Psalms for Chorus and Orchestra,
second movement

Igor Stravinsky   1930

177

Sonata for Flute and Piano,
first movement

Paul Hindemith   1936

Aeolian Harp

Henry Cowell   1923

Explanation of Symbols

All of the notes of the "Aeolian Harp" should be pressed down on the keys, without sounding, at the same time being played on the open strings of the piano with the other hand.

sw. indicates that the strings should be swept from the lowest to the highest note of the chord given, or if the arpeggio mark is given with a downward arrow, from the top to the bottom note of the chord.

pizz. indicates the string is to be plucked. Both sweeps and plucks are made with the flesh of the finger unless otherwise indicated.

"inside" indicates that the notes are to be played near the center of the string, inside the steel bar which runs parallel to the keyboard across the strings.

"outside" indicates that the notes are to be played outside this bar, near the tuning pegs.

Except where indicated, the pedal must NEVER BE DOWN while the strings are being swept; as soon as the sweep is made, the pedal should be put down, and held until the time is ready to begin a new sweep, when it must be released.

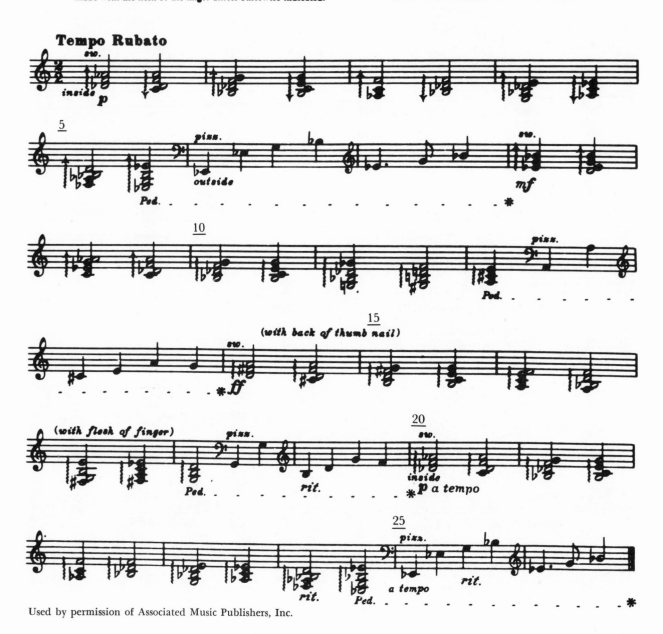

179

Symphony No. 3,
first movement, mm. 1–49

William Schuman 1942

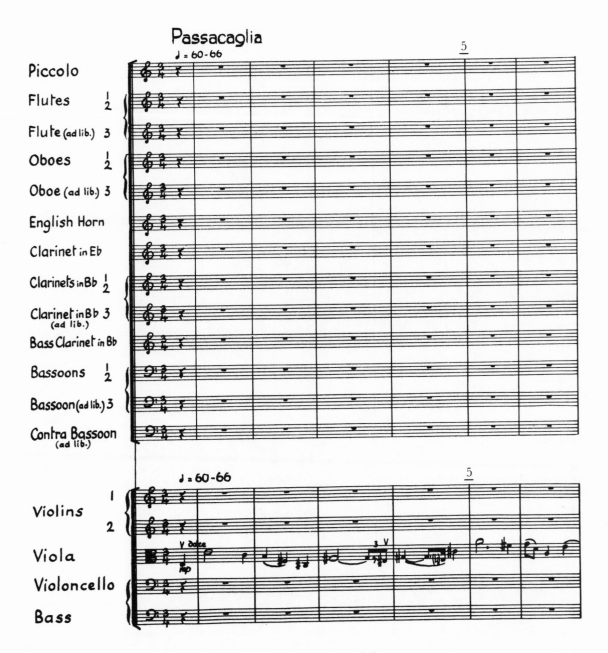

Nature, the Gentlest Mother

from *Twelve Poems by Emily Dickinson*

Aaron Copland 1951

293

Piano Piece

from *Five Piano Pieces* Op. 23
Arnold Schoenberg   1923

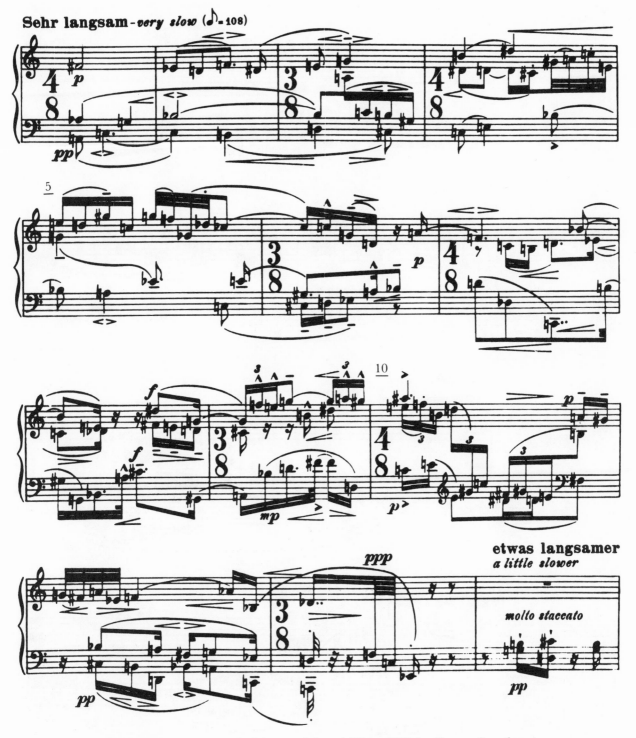

182

Piece for Orchestra
Op. 10 No. 3

Anton Webern   1913

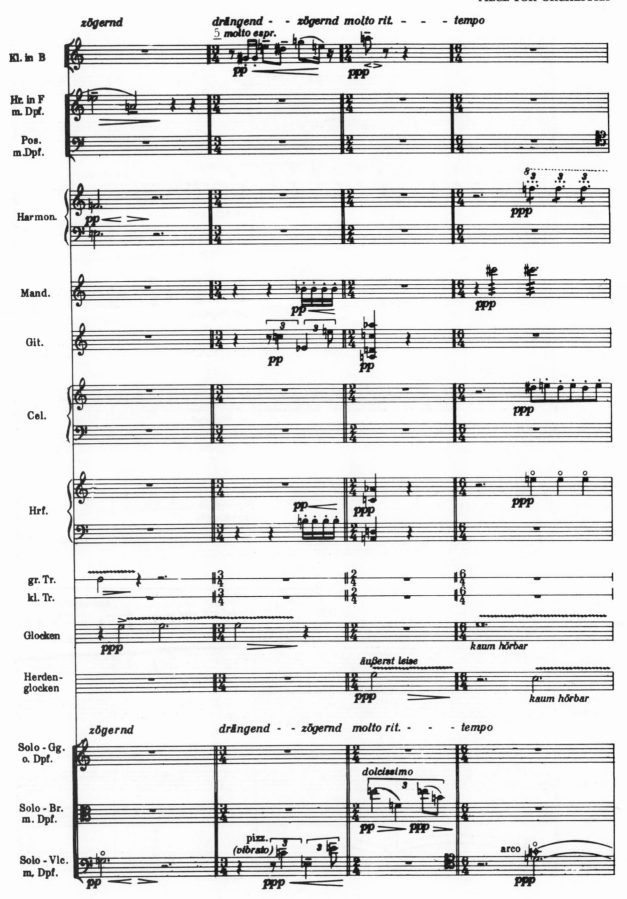

183

Density 21.5 for flute solo

Edgard Varèse   1936

Written in January, 1936, at the request of Georges Barrère for the inauguration of his platinum flute. Revised April, 1946. 21.5 is the density of platinum.

* Always strictly in time—follow metronomic indications.

** Notes marked + to be played softly, hitting the keys at the same time to produce a percussive effect.

Eight Etudes and a Fantasy

for Woodwind Quartet: No. 1

Elliott Carter   1950

Eight Etudes and a Fantasy

for Woodwind Quartet: No. 7

Elliott Carter   1950

VII

Intensely (♩ = 126)

Goethe Songs,
No. 1 for mezzo soprano and three clarinets

Luigi Dallapiccola   1953

Voice

Soprano Clarinet

Clarinet

Bass Clarinet

All instruments sound as written.

You may con-
ceal your-self in man-y guis-es, Yet, dear-ly lov'd one,
I will find you out; You

Goethe Songs, No. 2

Luigi Dallapiccola 1953

Goethe Songs, No. 4

Luigi Dallapiccola   1953

If — but wa-ter, spring-ing, gush-ing, If but cy- press would — tell

Fourth String Quartet

Op. 37, first movement, mm. 1–31

Arnold Schoenberg   1936

H̄ denotes the leading voice.

N̄ denotes a secondary voice.

Semi-Simple Variations

Milton Babbitt   1957

NOTE: Accidentals affect only those notes which they immediately precede.

SEMI-SIMPLE VARIATIONS